INDULGENCE

cookies

more than 40 crisp and crunchy recipes

THUNDER BAY
P·R·E·S·S

San Diego, California

Contents

Cover recipe on page 90

Wholesome

An abundance of fruit, nuts, and seeds star
in these nourishing delights.

Orange polenta cookies

MAKES 20–22

½ cup unsalted butter, softened
⅓ cup superfine sugar
1 teaspoon orange flower water
finely grated zest from 1 orange
2 eggs
1⅓ cups all-purpose flour
½ cup polenta

Preheat the oven to 400°F. Line two cookie sheets with parchment paper.

Combine the butter, sugar, orange flower water, and orange zest in a food processor, and process until light and creamy. Add the eggs and process until smooth. Add the flour and polenta, and pulse until a sticky dough forms.

Transfer the mixture to a piping bag fitted with a ¾-inch star nozzle. Pipe the mixture onto the prepared cookie sheets to form 2¾-inch crescents. Bake for 15 minutes, or until lightly golden around the edges. Allow to cool on the sheets for a few minutes, then transfer to a wire rack to cool completely.

Orange polenta cookies will keep, stored in an airtight container, for up to 3 days.

Fig and ginger cookies

MAKES 36

Preheat the oven to 350°F. Line two cookie sheets with parchment paper.

Cream the butter, sugar, and vanilla in a medium-sized bowl using electric beaters until pale and fluffy, then add the egg yolk and beat until just combined.

Transfer the butter mixture to a large bowl, add the figs and ginger, and stir to combine. Sift the flour into the mixture and add the baking soda and ground ginger. Stir with a wooden spoon until a soft dough forms.

Shape tablespoons of dough into balls, place on the prepared sheets 1½ inches apart, and flatten slightly. Bake for 10–12 minutes, or until lightly golden around the edges. Allow to cool on the sheets for a few minutes, then transfer to a wire rack to cool completely. Repeat with the remaining dough.

These cookies will keep, stored in an airtight container, for up to 4 days.

⅔ cup unsalted butter, softened
¾ cup soft brown sugar
1 teaspoon natural vanilla extract
1 egg yolk
½ cup chopped semi-dried figs
½ cup chopped candied ginger
1¾ cups all-purpose flour
½ teaspoon baking soda
1½ tablespoons ground ginger

Chunky chocolate and granola cookies

MAKES 36

½ cup unsalted butter, softened
1 cup soft brown sugar
1 teaspoon natural vanilla extract
1 egg
1 cup all-purpose flour
½ cup self-rising flour
½ teaspoon baking soda
⅓ cup unsweetened cocoa powder
½ cup unsweetened dried coconut
1 cup natural fruit and nut granola
1⅔ cups chopped bittersweet chocolate

Preheat the oven to 350°F. Line two cookie sheets with parchment paper.

Cream the butter, sugar, and vanilla in a medium-sized bowl using electric beaters until pale and fluffy, then add the egg and beat until just combined. In a separate bowl, sift together both flours, the baking soda, and the cocoa powder. Add to the butter mixture with the coconut, granola, and chocolate. Stir with a wooden spoon until a soft dough forms.

Shape tablespoons of dough into balls, place on the prepared sheets 2 inches apart, and flatten slightly. Bake for 12 minutes, or until crisp on top and lightly golden. Allow to cool on the sheets for a few minutes, then transfer to a wire rack to cool completely. Repeat with the remaining dough.

These cookies will keep, stored in an airtight container, for up to 2 weeks.

Fennel wafers

MAKES 40

Lightly grease a cookie sheet and line with parchment
paper. In a small bowl, combine the sugar, sesame
seeds, and fennel seeds. In a separate, large bowl, sift
the flour and a pinch of salt, and make a well in the
center. Add the oil, beer, and liqueur, and mix with a
large metal spoon until the dough comes together.

Transfer the dough onto a lightly floured surface and
knead until it is smooth and elastic. Wrap the dough
in plastic wrap and refrigerate for 30 minutes.

Preheat the oven to 400°F. Divide the dough in half and
roll out each portion between two sheets of parchment
paper as thinly as possible. Stamp rounds out of the
dough using a 1½-inch round cookie cutter—you should
get about 40 rounds.

Sprinkle the dough rounds with the sugar mixture,
then gently roll a rolling pin over the top of them so
that the seeds adhere to the dough.

Transfer the rounds to the prepared sheet and bake for
6–8 minutes, then place the wafers under a hot broiler
for 1–2 minutes to caramelize the sugar, taking care not
to burn them. Transfer to a wire rack to cool completely.
Repeat with the remaining dough.

These wafers will keep, stored in an airtight
container, for up to 2 weeks.

¼ cup superfine sugar
2 tablespoons sesame seeds
2 tablespoons fennel seeds
1½ cups all-purpose flour
¼ cup olive oil
¼ cup beer
1 tablespoon anise liqueur

Walnut crisps

1 egg
1 egg yolk
½ cup superfine sugar
½ teaspoon natural vanilla extract
2 tablespoons all-purpose flour
1¼ cups chopped golden walnuts

Preheat the oven to 325°F. Line two cookie sheets with parchment paper.

Using electric beaters, beat the egg, egg yolk, sugar, and vanilla in a medium-sized bowl until combined. Sift the flour into the egg mixture. Stir with a wooden spoon until smooth, then fold in the walnuts.

Shape rounded teaspoons of dough and place them well apart on the prepared sheets. Flatten slightly and bake for 15–17 minutes, or until lightly golden and crisp. Allow to cool on the sheets for a few minutes, then transfer to a wire rack to cool completely.

The crisps will keep, stored in an airtight container, for up to 2 weeks.

Banana spice cookies

MAKES 36

Preheat the oven to 325°F. Line two cookie sheets with parchment paper.

Cream the butter, sugar, and vanilla in a medium-sized bowl using electric beaters until pale and fluffy, then add the egg yolk and beat until just combined. Add the banana chips and stir to combine. Sift the flours into the butter mixture, and add the pumpkin pie spice and coconut. Stir with a wooden spoon until a soft dough forms.

Shape tablespoons of dough into balls and place on the prepared sheets 1½ inches apart. Flatten the balls slightly, then press a clove into the top of each one. Bake for 12 minutes, or until lightly golden around the edges. Allow to cool on the sheets for a few minutes, then transfer to a wire rack to cool completely. Repeat with the remaining dough.

Banana spice cookies will keep, stored in an airtight container, for up to 1 week.

¾ cup unsalted butter, softened
1 cup superfine sugar
1 teaspoon natural vanilla extract
1 egg yolk
1 cup dried banana chips, chopped
1 cup all-purpose flour
1 cup self-rising flour
2 teaspoons pumpkin pie spice
½ cup unsweetened dried coconut
2 tablespoons whole cloves, to garnish

Cranberry and hazelnut refrigerator cookies

MAKES 50

⅔ cup plus 1 tablespoon unsalted butter, softened
1 cup confectioners' sugar
2 egg yolks
2 teaspoons lemon juice
1½ cups all-purpose flour
1 cup ground hazelnuts
1½ cups sweetened dried cranberries
½ cup poppy seeds

Cream the butter and sugar in a medium-sized bowl using electric beaters until pale and fluffy, then add the egg yolks and lemon juice, and beat until just combined. Sift the flour into the butter mixture and add the ground hazelnuts. Stir well with a wooden spoon, then stir in the cranberries. Divide the mixture in half.

Scatter half the poppy seeds over a 12-inch long piece of foil. Place half the mixture on the work surface and form it into a 8¼-inch long sausage shape. Transfer the dough to the foil, rolling the dough in the poppy seeds to coat, then roll tightly in the foil to form a neat cylinder, twisting the ends tight. Repeat with the remaining dough and poppy seeds and another piece of foil. Refrigerate the dough for a minimum of 4 hours.

Preheat the oven to 325°F and lightly grease two cookie sheets.

Remove the foil and cut the dough into ⅜-inch slices. Place the rounds on the prepared sheets and bake for 12–15 minutes, or until firm and lightly golden. Cool on the sheets for a few minutes, then transfer to a wire rack to cool completely.

These cookies will keep, stored in an airtight container, for up to 1 week.

Macadamia and white chocolate cookies

MAKES 25

1⅓ cups macadamia nuts
1 egg
¾ cup soft brown sugar
2 tablespoons sugar
1 teaspoon natural vanilla extract
½ cup olive oil
½ cup all-purpose flour
¼ cup self-rising flour
¼ teaspoon ground cinnamon
½ cup unsweetened shredded coconut
¾ cup white chocolate chips

Preheat the oven to 350°F. Place the macadamias on a cookie sheet and bake for 5 minutes, or until lightly toasted. Cool and roughly chop into small pieces with a large sharp knife.

Using electric beaters, beat the egg and sugars in a medium-sized bowl until light and fluffy, then add the vanilla and oil. Sift the flours into the egg mixture and add the cinnamon, coconut, toasted macadamias, and chocolate chips. Mix well with a wooden spoon, then refrigerate for 30 minutes.

Lightly grease two cookie sheets and line with parchment paper. Shape tablespoons of dough into balls and place on the cookie sheets, pressing the mixture together with your fingertips if crumbly. Bake for 12–15 minutes, or until lightly golden around the edges. Allow to cool on the sheets for a few minutes, then transfer to a wire rack to cool completely.

These cookies will keep, stored in an airtight container, for up to 1 week.

VARIATION: Bittersweet chocolate chips can be used instead of white chocolate.

Rosemary and raisin cookies

MAKES 24

½ cup unsalted butter, softened
½ cup superfine sugar
½ cup soft brown sugar
½ teaspoon natural vanilla extract
1 egg
2 cups all-purpose flour
1 teaspoon baking powder
½ teaspoon ground nutmeg
1 tablespoon chopped rosemary, plus 24 small sprigs, to garnish
1 cup raisins

Preheat the oven to 350°F. Line two cookie sheets with parchment paper.

Cream the butter, sugars, and vanilla in a small bowl using electric beaters until pale and fluffy, then add the egg and beat until just combined. Transfer the mixture to a large bowl. Sift the flour into the butter mixture, then and add the baking powder, nutmeg, rosemary, and raisins. Stir with a wooden spoon until a soft dough forms.

Shape tablespoons of dough into balls, place on the prepared sheets 2 inches apart, and flatten slightly to make 1½-inch rounds. Garnish the top of each with a rosemary sprig and bake for 12–13 minutes, or until lightly golden. Allow to cool on the sheets for a few minutes, then transfer to a wire rack to cool completely.

These cookies will keep, stored in an airtight container, for up to 5 days.

Peach, cinnamon, and almond cookies

MAKES 30

Preheat the oven to 375°F. Line two cookie sheets with parchment paper.

Cream the butter, sugar, and vanilla in a medium-sized bowl using electric beaters until pale and fluffy, then add the egg and beat until just combined. Add the peach and stir to combine. Sift the flour and add to the mixture along with the baking powder, cinnamon, and ground almonds. Stir with a wooden spoon until a soft dough forms.

Shape tablespoons of dough into balls and place on the prepared sheets 2 inches apart. Place a blanched almond on top of each, gently pressing into the dough, and flatten slightly to make 1½-inch rounds. Bake for 12 minutes, or until lightly golden around the edges. Allow to cool on the sheets for a few minutes, then transfer to a wire rack to cool completely. Repeat with the remaining dough.

These cookies will keep, stored in an airtight container, for up to 1 week.

⅔ cup unsalted butter, softened
1 cup superfine sugar
½ teaspoon natural vanilla extract
1 egg
⅔ cup dried peaches, finely chopped
1¾ cups all-purpose flour
1 teaspoon baking powder
1 teaspoon ground cinnamon
½ cup ground almonds
⅓ cup blanched almonds, to garnish

Trail mix and honey cookies

MAKES 20

2 teaspoons finely grated lime zest
¼ cup honey
2 egg whites
½ teaspoon natural vanilla extract
¼ cup all-purpose flour
⅓ cup finely sliced candied papaya
2 tablespoons finely sliced candied pineapple
¼ cup flaked almonds
¼ cup pistachio nuts, chopped
1 tablespoon pumpkin seeds
2 teaspoons sesame seeds
¾ cup unsweetened flaked coconut
¼ cup unsweetened dried coconut

Preheat the oven to 325°F. Line two cookie sheets with parchment paper.

Combine the lime zest, honey, egg whites, and vanilla in a medium-sized bowl, and whisk until frothy. In a separate, large bowl, sift the flour and add the papaya, pineapple, almonds, pistachios, pumpkin seeds, sesame seeds, and coconut. Make a well in the center, then add the egg white mixture. Stir with a wooden spoon until a soft dough forms.

Shape tablespoons of the mixture into balls, place on the prepared sheets 1½ inches apart and flatten slightly. Bake for 15 minutes, or until they are lightly golden around the edges. Allow to cool on the sheets for a few minutes, then transfer to a wire rack to cool completely.

Trail mix and honey cookies are best served on the day they are made.

Malted milk and oat cookies

MAKES 26

Preheat the oven to 350°F. Line two cookie sheets with parchment paper.

Sift the flour in a large bowl and add the oats, sugar, milk powder, and the coconut. Mix together and make a well in the center.

Place the honey, 1 tablespoon hot water, and the butter in a small saucepan. Stir over low heat until the butter has melted. Pour the butter mixture into the well in the dry ingredients and stir with a wooden spoon until a soft dough forms.

Shape tablespoons of dough into balls, place well apart on the prepared sheets and flatten slightly. Bake for 12–15 minutes, or until golden brown around the edges. Allow to cool on the sheets for a few minutes, then transfer to a wire rack to cool completely. Repeat with the remaining dough.

These cookies will keep, stored in an airtight container, for up to 1 week.

1 cup self-rising flour
1 cup rolled oats
¾ cup superfine sugar
⅓ cup malted milk powder
¾ cup unsweetened dried coconut
2 tablespoons honey
½ cup plus 2 tablespoons unsalted butter

Date and sesame cookies

⅔ cup unsalted butter, softened
1 cup soft brown sugar
1 teaspoon natural vanilla extract
1 egg
2 teaspoons sesame oil
1 cup chopped dates
2 cups all-purpose flour
1 teaspoon baking powder
⅓ cup sesame seeds

Preheat the oven to 350°F. Line two cookie sheets with parchment paper.

Cream the butter, sugar, and vanilla in a medium-sized bowl using electric beaters until pale and fluffy, then add the egg and sesame oil, beating until just combined. Add the dates and stir to combine. Sift in the flour and baking powder, and stir with a wooden spoon to form a soft dough.

Place the sesame seeds in a small bowl. Shape tablespoons of the dough into balls and press one side down into the sesame seeds. Place on the prepared sheets, sesame side up, 2 inches apart, and then flatten slightly to make 1½-inch rounds. Bake for 12 minutes, or until lightly golden. Allow to cool on the sheets for a few minutes, then transfer to a wire rack to cool completely. Repeat with the remaining dough.

These cookies will keep, stored in an airtight container, for up to 5 days.

Fig oaties

MAKES 30

Preheat the oven to 350°F. Cream the butter and sugar in a medium-sized bowl using electric beaters until pale and fluffy, then add the egg and milk and beat until smooth. Stir in ½ teaspoon salt, cinnamon, and baking soda. Add the sesame seeds, figs, and oats. Sift the flour and fold into the mixture with a wooden spoon.

Shape tablespoons of the dough into balls and place well apart on two ungreased cookie sheets. Flatten slightly and top with a slice of fig. Bake for 15–20 minutes, or until lightly golden around the edges. Allow to cool on the sheets for a few minutes, then transfer to a wire rack to cool completely.

Fig oaties will keep, stored in an airtight container, for up to 5 days.

½ cup unsalted butter, softened
1 cup superfine sugar
1 egg
2 tablespoons milk
½ teaspoon ground cinnamon
½ teaspoon baking soda
¾ cup sesame seeds
1½ cups chopped dried figs
1¼ cups rolled oats
1¼ cups all-purpose flour
6 dried figs, sliced, to garnish

Plain Jane

Simple these may be, but there's nothing ordinary
about these cookie jar essentials.

Jam thumbprints

MAKES 45

1 cup unsalted butter, softened
heaping 1 cup confectioners' sugar
1 egg yolk, lightly beaten
⅓ cup cream cheese, softened and cut into chunks
1½ teaspoons natural vanilla extract
1 teaspoon finely grated lemon zest
2¾ cups all-purpose flour
¼ teaspoon baking powder
½ teaspoon baking soda
2 tablespoons each apricot, blueberry and raspberry jam

Preheat the oven to 350°F and grease three cookie sheets.

Cream the butter, sugar, and the egg yolk in a bowl using electric beaters until pale and fluffy, then beat in the cream cheese, vanilla, and lemon zest until smooth. Sift the flour, baking powder, baking soda, and ¼ teaspoon salt into a large bowl and, using a wooden spoon, gradually stir in the butter mixture until a soft dough forms. Set aside for 5–10 minutes, or until the dough firms up.

Shape tablespoons of the dough into balls, place on the prepared sheets well apart and flatten slightly to make 1½-inch rounds. Make a small indent in the center of each and spoon about ¼ teaspoon of apricot jam into one-third of the cookies, ¼ teaspoon blueberry jam into one-third, and ¼ teaspoon of raspberry jam into the remaining one-third of the cookies. Bake for 10–12 minutes, or until lightly golden. Allow to cool on the sheets for a few minutes, then transfer to a wire rack to cool completely.

These cookies are best eaten the same day but will keep, stored in an airtight container, for up to 2 days.

Crackle cookies

MAKES 60

½ cup chopped bittersweet chocolate
½ cup unsalted butter, softened
2 cups soft brown sugar
1 teaspoon natural vanilla extract
2 eggs
⅓ cup milk
2¾ cups all-purpose flour
2 tablespoons unsweetened cocoa powder
2 teaspoons baking powder
¼ teaspoon pumpkin pie spice
⅔ cup chopped pecans
confectioners' sugar, to coat

Place the chocolate in a heatproof bowl over a saucepan of simmering water, ensuring the bowl doesn't touch the water. Stir until the chocolate is melted. Set aside to cool for 5 minutes.

Cream the butter, sugar, and vanilla in a medium-sized bowl using electric beaters until pale and fluffy, then add the eggs, one at a time, beating until just combined. Add the melted chocolate and milk, and stir to combine.

Sift the flour, cocoa, baking powder, pumpkin pie spice, and a pinch of salt into the butter mixture and mix well. Stir the pecans through. Refrigerate for at least 3 hours, or overnight.

Preheat the oven to 350°F. Lightly grease two cookie sheets. Roll tablespoons of the mixture into balls and roll each in the confectioners' sugar to coat. Place well apart on the sheets. Bake for 20–25 minutes, or until lightly browned. Allow to cool on the sheets for a few minutes, then transfer to a wire rack to cool completely. Repeat with the remaining mixture.

These cookies will keep, stored in an airtight container, for up to 2 days.

Maple brown sugar cookies

MAKES 48

½ cup plus 1 tablespoon unsalted butter, softened
1 cup soft brown sugar
⅓ cup maple syrup
1 egg yolk
2 cups all-purpose flour
½ teaspoon baking soda
¼ teaspoon ground cinnamon
¼ teaspoon ground cardamom
1 cup confectioners' sugar, sifted
1½ tablespoons maple syrup, extra
½ teaspoon natural vanilla extract

Preheat the oven to 350°F. Line two cookie sheets with parchment paper.

Cream the butter and sugar in a medium-sized bowl using electric beaters until pale and fluffy, then add the maple syrup and egg yolk, beating until just combined. Sift in the flour, baking soda, cinnamon, and cardamom, and stir with a wooden spoon to form a soft dough. Shape the dough into a flat disk, cover with plastic wrap, and refrigerate for 20 minutes.

Roll out the dough between two pieces of parchment paper to ¼ inch thick. Cut the dough into rings using a 2-inch round cookie cutter, re-rolling the dough scraps and cutting more circles. Place on the prepared sheets 1½ inches apart and bake for 8 minutes, or until lightly golden. Allow to cool on the sheets for a few minutes, then transfer to a wire rack to cool completely. Repeat with the remaining dough.

To make the maple syrup frosting, place the confectioners' sugar, extra maple syrup, and vanilla in a medium-sized bowl, and stir to combine. Add enough water to make a smooth, thick, runny consistency. When the cookies are completely cool, drizzle with the maple syrup frosting.

These cookies will keep, stored in an airtight container, for up to 3 weeks.

Chocolate chip cookies

MAKES 16

½ cup unsalted butter, softened
1 cup soft brown sugar
1 teaspoon natural vanilla extract
1 egg, lightly beaten
1 tablespoon milk
1¾ cups all-purpose flour
1 teaspoon baking powder
1½ cups bittersweet chocolate chips

Preheat the oven to 350°F. Line a large cookie sheet with parchment paper.

Cream the butter and sugar in a large bowl using electric beaters until pale and fluffy, then add the vanilla and egg, beating until just combined. Add the milk and stir to combine. Sift in the flour and baking powder, stir in the bittersweet chocolate chips, and stir with a wooden spoon to form a soft dough.

Shape tablespoons of dough into balls, place on the prepared sheet 1½ inches apart, and flatten slightly. Bake for 15 minutes, or until lightly golden around the edges. Allow to cool on the sheet for a few minutes, then transfer to a wire rack to cool completely.

These cookies will keep, stored in an airtight container, for up to 2 days.

Crumbly cashew cookies

MAKES 36

½ cup plus 1 tablespoon unsalted butter,
softened
⅔ cup superfine sugar
1 teaspoon natural vanilla extract
1 egg yolk
1 cup unsalted cashews, finely chopped
2 cups all-purpose flour

Preheat the oven to 325°F. Line two cookie sheets with parchment paper.

Cream the butter, sugar, and vanilla in a medium-sized bowl using electric beaters until pale and fluffy, then add the egg yolk and beat until just combined. Add the cashews and sift in the flour. Stir with a wooden spoon until a soft dough forms.

Shape tablespoons of dough into balls, place on the prepared sheets 1½ inches apart, and flatten slightly with a fork dipped in flour. Bake for 8–10 minutes, or until lightly golden around the edges. Allow to cool on the sheets for a few minutes, then transfer to a wire rack to cool completely. Repeat with the remaining dough.

Crumbly cashew cookies will keep, stored in an airtight container, for up to 2 weeks.

Ginger fingers

MAKES 25

¾ cup chopped macadamia nuts
1 cup unsalted butter, softened
⅓ cup superfine sugar
½ cup candied ginger, chopped
2 cups all-purpose flour
½ cup rice flour
superfine sugar, to sprinkle

Preheat the oven to 300°F. Line a large cookie sheet with parchment paper. Lay the macadamias on another cookie sheet and toast for 3–5 minutes, or until lightly golden. Set aside to cool.

Cream the butter and sugar in a medium-sized bowl using electric beaters until pale and fluffy. Mix in the ginger and nuts. Sift in the flours and stir with a wooden spoon to form a dough.

Gather the dough into a ball and roll out to a ½-inch thick rectangle. Cut into 1¼ x 2¾-inch fingers. Place on the prepared sheet and sprinkle with the superfine sugar. Bake for 35 minutes, or until the ginger fingers are pale golden underneath. Allow to cool on the sheet for a few minutes, then transfer to a wire rack to cool completely.

Ginger fingers will keep, stored in an airtight container, for up to 2 days.

Pecan praline cookies

MAKES 24

½ cup superfine sugar
½ cup unsalted butter, softened
¾ cup superfine sugar, extra
1 teaspoon natural vanilla extract
1 egg yolk
2 cups all-purpose flour
1 teaspoon baking powder
1½ cups whole pecans

Preheat the oven to 350°F. Line two cookie sheets with parchment paper.

To make the praline, combine the superfine sugar and 1 tablespoon water in a small saucepan, stirring over low heat until the sugar is dissolved. Use a pastry brush to brush down any excess sugar on the side of the saucepan. Once the sugar is dissolved, stop stirring and continue cooking until the liquid becomes a golden caramel color. Pour this toffee onto one of the prepared sheets, spreading it out evenly. Allow to cool and harden, then break into pieces. Process in a food processor until finely chopped. Re-line the cookie sheet with parchment paper.

Cream the butter, extra sugar, and vanilla in a medium-sized bowl using electric beaters until pale and fluffy, then add the egg yolk, beating until just combined. Add the finely chopped praline and stir to combine. Sift in the flour and baking powder, and stir with a wooden spoon to form a soft dough.

Shape tablespoons of the dough into small logs and press a pecan into the center of each. Place on the prepared sheets 1½ inches apart and bake for 12–15 minutes, or until lightly golden around the edges. Allow to cool on the sheets for a few minutes, then transfer to a wire rack to cool completely.

These cookies will keep, stored in an airtight container, for up to 2 weeks.

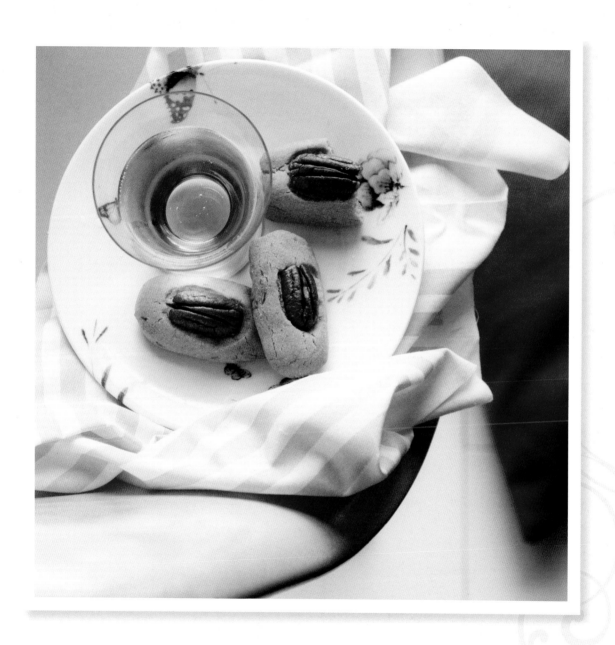

Cinnamon circles

MAKES 25

3½ tablespoons unsalted butter, softened
⅓ cup superfine sugar
½ teaspoon natural vanilla extract
⅔ cup all-purpose flour
1 tablespoon milk
2 tablespoons superfine sugar, extra
½ teaspoon ground cinnamon

Preheat the oven to 350°F. Line two cookie sheets with parchment paper.

Cream the butter and sugar in a medium-sized bowl using electric beaters until pale and fluffy, then stir in the vanilla. Sift in the flour and add the milk. Stir with a wooden spoon to form a soft dough, gather into a ball and place on a sheet of parchment paper.

Press the dough out to a log shape, 10 inches long and 1¼ inches thick. Roll in the paper and twist the ends to seal. Refrigerate for 20 minutes, or until firm.

Cut the log into rounds ½ inch thick. Sift the extra superfine sugar and cinnamon onto a plate and roll each cookie in the sugar mixture, coating well. Lay well apart on the prepared sheets and bake for 20 minutes, or until lightly golden around the edges. Allow to cool on the sheets for a few minutes, then transfer to a wire rack to cool completely.

These cookies will keep, stored in an airtight container, for up to 5 days.

plain jane

Marble cookies

1⅓ cups chopped bittersweet chocolate
½ cup unsalted butter, softened
1 cup superfine sugar
1 teaspoon natural vanilla extract
1 egg yolk
2 tablespoons milk
2 cups all-purpose flour
½ teaspoon baking powder

Preheat the oven to 350°F. Line two cookie sheets with parchment paper.

Place the chocolate in a heatproof bowl over a saucepan of simmering water, ensuring the bowl doesn't touch the water. Stir until the chocolate has melted. Set aside to cool for 5 minutes.

Cream the butter, sugar, and vanilla in a medium-sized bowl using electric beaters until pale and fluffy, then add the egg yolk and milk, beating until just combined. Sift in the flour and baking powder, and stir with a wooden spoon to form a soft dough.

Make a well in the center of the dough and pour in the chocolate. Using a knife, gently fold through the chocolate to give a rippled effect, being careful not to overmix.

Shape tablespoons of the dough into balls, place on the prepared sheets 2 inches apart and flatten slightly. Bake for 12–15 minutes, or until lightly golden around the edges. Allow to cool on the sheets for a few minutes, then transfer to a wire rack to cool completely. Repeat with the remaining dough.

These cookies will keep, stored in an airtight container, for up to 1 week.

Anise drops

MAKES 30

Preheat the oven to 350°F. Line two cookie sheets with parchment paper.

Cream the butter, sugar, vanilla, and anise in a medium-sized bowl using electric beaters until pale and fluffy, then add the egg yolk, honey, and milk, beating until just combined. Sift in the flours and baking powder and stir with a wooden spoon to form a soft dough.

Shape tablespoons of dough into balls, place on the prepared sheets 2 inches apart, and flatten slightly. Bake for 10–15 minutes, or until lightly golden around the edges. Allow to cool on the sheets for a few minutes, then transfer to a wire rack to cool completely. Repeat with the remaining dough.

These cookies will keep, stored in an airtight container, for up to 5 days.

¾ cup unsalted butter, softened
½ cup superfine sugar
1 teaspoon natural vanilla extract
1 teaspoon anise extract
1 egg yolk
2 tablespoons honey
1 tablespoon milk
2 cups all-purpose flour
½ cup rice flour
1½ teaspoons baking powder
1 teaspoon aniseeds

Classic shortbread

MAKES 16 WEDGES

scant 1 cup unsalted butter, softened
½ cup superfine sugar, plus extra for dusting
1¾ cups all-purpose flour
⅔ cup rice flour

Lightly grease two cookie sheets. Cream the butter and sugar in a medium-sized bowl using electric beaters until pale and fluffy. Sift in the flours and a pinch of salt and stir with a wooden spoon until it resembles fine breadcrumbs. Transfer to a lightly floured work surface and knead gently to form a soft dough. Cover with plastic wrap and refrigerate for 30 minutes.

Preheat the oven to 375°F. Divide the dough in half and roll out one half on a lightly floured work surface to form an 8-inch round. Carefully transfer to one of the prepared sheets. Using a sharp knife, score the surface of the dough into eight equal wedges, prick the surface lightly with a fork and, using your fingers, press the edge to form a fluted effect. Repeat using the remaining dough to make a second round. Lightly dust the shortbreads with the extra sugar.

Bake for 18–20 minutes, or until the shortbreads are lightly golden. Remove from the oven and while still hot, follow the score marks and cut into wedges. Cool on the cookie sheets for 5 minutes, then transfer to a wire rack.

These shortbreads will keep, stored in an airtight container, for up to 1 week.

TIP: While shortbread can be made with all-purpose flour alone, adding rice flour produces a lighter result.

Chocolate shortbread

MAKES 65

1 cup chopped bittersweet chocolate
1 cup unsalted butter, softened
½ cup superfine sugar
2½ cups all-purpose flour
2 tablespoons unsweetened cocoa powder
1 tablespoon drinking chocolate

Preheat the oven to 325°F. Lightly grease two cookie sheets.

Place the chocolate in a heatproof bowl over a saucepan of simmering water, ensuring the bowl doesn't touch the water. Stir until the chocolate has melted. Set aside to cool for 5 minutes.

Cream the butter and sugar in a medium-sized bowl using electric beaters until pale and fluffy, then add the melted chocolate. Sift in the flour and stir with a wooden spoon to form a soft dough.

Shape tablespoons of the dough into balls, place on the prepared sheets well apart and flatten slightly. Bake for 12–15 minutes. Allow to cool on the sheets for a few minutes, then transfer to a wire rack to cool completely. Repeat with the remaining dough.

Just before serving, sift the combined cocoa and drinking chocolate over the shortbread to dust.

These shortbreads will keep, stored in an airtight container, for up to 1 week.

Custard dream stars

MAKES 30

¾ cup unsalted butter, softened
⅓ cup confectioners' sugar
1 teaspoon natural vanilla extract
1 cup all-purpose flour
⅓ cup instant custard powder
small sugar decorations

Preheat the oven to 350°F. Line two cookie sheets with parchment paper.

Cream the butter, sugar, and vanilla in a medium-sized bowl using electric beaters until pale and fluffy. Sift in the flour and custard powder, and stir with a wooden spoon to form a soft dough, being careful not to overmix.

Transfer the mixture to a piping bag fitted with a ⅝-inch star nozzle. Pipe the mixture well apart onto the prepared cookie sheets to form star shapes, about 1½ inches in diameter. Place a sugar decoration in the center of each star. Refrigerate for 20 minutes.

Bake for 12–15 minutes, or until lightly golden, taking care not to burn. Allow to cool on the sheets for a few minutes, then transfer to a wire rack to cool completely.

Custard dream stars will keep, stored in an airtight container, for up to 5 days.

NOTE: You can buy small sugar decorations from most grocery stores.

Cardamom crescents

MAKES 30

½ cup slivered almonds
1 cup unsalted butter, softened
3 tablespoons confectioners' sugar, sifted
2 tablespoons brandy
1 teaspoon finely grated lime zest
2½ cups all-purpose flour
1 teaspoon ground cardamom
confectioners' sugar, extra, to dust
  and to store (optional)

Preheat the oven to 350°F. Line two cookie sheets with parchment paper. Put the almonds on another cookie sheet and bake for 5 minutes, or until lightly golden. Allow to cool and finely chop.

Cream the butter and sugar in a medium-sized bowl using electric beaters until pale and fluffy, then mix in the brandy, lime zest, and the toasted almonds. Sift in the flour and cardamom, and stir with a wooden spoon to form a soft dough.

Shape tablespoons of the dough into small crescents and place on the prepared sheets well apart. Bake for 15–20 minutes, or until lightly golden. Allow to cool on the sheets for a few minutes, then transfer to a wire rack to cool completely.

To serve, sift over some of the confectioners' sugar to cover the crescents completely. If storing the crescents, place in a tin or plastic box and cover entirely with the remaining confectioners' sugar.

The crescents will keep, stored in an airtight container, for up to 5 days.

Coffee wafers

¾ cup unsalted butter, softened
¾ cup superfine sugar
¼ cup dark brown sugar
1 teaspoon natural vanilla extract
1 egg yolk
1 tablespoon milk
¼ cup strong espresso coffee
3 cups all-purpose flour
1 cup confectioners' sugar, sifted
1 tablespoon espresso coffee, extra
coffee beans, to garnish

Preheat the oven to 350°F. Line two cookie sheets with parchment paper.

Cream the butter and sugars in a large bowl using electric beaters until pale and fluffy, then add the vanilla, egg yolk, milk, and coffee, beating until just combined. Sift in the flour and stir with a wooden spoon to form a soft dough.

Turn the dough out onto a lightly floured work surface and knead gently until the mixture comes together. Divide the mixture into two and roll each portion between two pieces of parchment paper to ¼ inch thick. Cut the dough into rounds using a 2-inch round cookie cutter, re-rolling the dough scraps and cutting out more rounds. Place on the prepared sheets 1¼ inches apart and bake for 10 minutes, or until golden around the edges. Allow to cool on the sheets for a few minutes, then transfer to a wire rack to cool completely. Repeat with the remaining dough.

To make the coffee frosting, place the confectioners' sugar and coffee in a small bowl and stir until smooth. Using a spoon, spread a circle of frosting on top of each wafer and top with coffee beans.

These wafers will keep, stored in an airtight container, for up to 2 weeks.

Honey snaps

MAKES 24

Preheat the oven to 350°F. Line two cookie sheets with parchment paper.

Cream the butter and sugars in a medium-sized bowl using electric beaters until pale and fluffy, then add the honey, egg yolk, and vanilla, beating until just combined. Sift in the flour and baking soda, and stir with a wooden spoon to form a soft dough.

Shape tablespoons of the dough into logs, place on the prepared sheets 2 inches apart, and flatten slightly. Bake for 10 minutes, or until lightly golden around the edges. Allow to cool on the sheets for a few minutes, then transfer to a wire rack to cool completely.

To make the frosting, place the confectioners' sugar in a medium-sized bowl. Add enough lemon juice to make a smooth and spreadable consistency. Once the snaps are completely cooled, spread the tops with the frosting.

Honey snaps will keep, stored in an airtight container, for up to 3 weeks.

½ cup unsalted butter, softened
¼ cup superfine sugar
¼ cup soft brown sugar
⅓ cup honey
1 egg yolk
1 teaspoon natural vanilla extract
2 cups all-purpose flour
½ teaspoon baking soda
1 cup confectioners' sugar
1–2 tablespoons lemon juice

Chocolate mud cookies

MAKES 36

1²⁄₃ cups chopped bittersweet chocolate
½ cup unsalted butter, softened
1 cup soft brown sugar
1 teaspoon natural vanilla extract
1 egg
1½ cups all-purpose flour
⅓ cup unsweetened cocoa powder

Preheat the oven to 350°F. Line two cookie sheets with parchment paper.

Place the chocolate in a food processor and pulse until finely chopped, then set aside.

Cream the butter, sugar, and vanilla in a medium-sized bowl using electric beaters until pale and fluffy, then add the egg, beating until just combined. Sift in the flour and cocoa, add the chopped chocolate, and stir with a wooden spoon to form a soft dough.

Shape tablespoons of the dough into balls, place on the prepared sheets well apart, and flatten into 1¾-inch rounds. Bake for 9 minutes. Allow to cool on the sheets for a few minutes, then transfer to a wire rack to cool completely. Repeat with the remaining dough.

These cookies will keep, stored in an airtight container, for up to 1 week.

Dipped & drizzled

These indulgent morsels are the perfect offering
for that special occasion . . . or just because.

Lime and coconut shortbreads

MAKES 25

2 cups all-purpose flour
⅓ cup confectioners' sugar
¾ cup unsweetened dried coconut
2 teaspoons finely grated lime zest
¾ cup plus 1 tablespoon unsalted butter, cubed and chilled
1 tablespoon lime juice
1 cup confectioners' sugar, extra
2 tablespoons lime juice, extra, strained

Preheat the oven to 350°F. Line two cookie sheets with parchment paper.

Sift the flour and confectioners' sugar into a bowl and stir in the coconut and lime zest. Add the butter and rub in with your fingertips until crumbly. Add the lime juice and cut into the flour mixture using a flat-bladed knife.

Gather the dough into a ball and roll out on a lightly floured work surface to ¼ inch thick. Using a 2-inch cookie cutter, cut into rounds. Lay well apart on the prepared sheets and bake for 15–20 minutes, or until very lightly golden. Allow to cool on the sheets for a few minutes, then transfer to a wire rack to cool completely.

To make the frosting, sift the extra confectioners' sugar into a small heatproof bowl, add the extra lime juice, and place over a saucepan of simmering water. Stir until smooth. Spoon a little frosting onto each shortbread, stirring the frosting in the bowl occasionally to prevent it from hardening, and spread evenly. Leave the shortbread on the wire rack to set.

These shortbread will keep, stored in an airtight container, for up to 5 days.

Spice cookies

½ cup unsalted butter, softened
⅓ cup soft brown sugar
1 egg
1 cup all-purpose flour
1 cup rice flour
1 teaspoon baking powder
1 teaspoon ground cinnamon
1 teaspoon pumpkin pie spice
1 teaspoon ground ginger
¼ cup raspberry jam

Ginger glacé frosting
1 cup confectioners' sugar
½ teaspoon ground ginger
1 tablespoon plus 1 teaspoon unsalted butter

Line two cookie sheets with parchment paper. Cream the butter and sugar in a medium-sized bowl using electric beaters until pale and fluffy, then add the egg, beating until just combined. Sift in the flours and baking powder, add the spices, and stir with a wooden spoon until smooth. Cover with plastic wrap and chill for about 30 minutes.

Preheat the oven to 350°F. Roll out the dough between two pieces of parchment paper to ¼ inch thick. Cut out the dough using a 2-inch fluted round cookie cutter, re-rolling the dough scraps and cutting more rounds. Place on the prepared sheets well apart and bake for 12–15 minutes, or until lightly golden. Allow to cool on the sheets for a few minutes, then transfer to a wire rack to cool completely.

To make the ginger glacé frosting, sift the confectioners' sugar and ginger into a bowl and mix together with the butter and 1 tablespoon boiling water. Sandwich the cookies with jam and spread on the frosting.

These cookies will keep, stored in an airtight container, for up to 5 days.

Citrus poppy seed cookies

MAKES 36

½ cup unsalted butter, softened
¾ cup superfine sugar
1 teaspoon natural vanilla extract
1 tablespoon finely grated orange zest
1 tablespoon finely grated lime zest
1 tablespoon orange juice
1 tablespoon lime juice
2 cups all-purpose flour
¼ teaspoon baking powder
2 tablespoons poppy seeds

Cream the butter, sugar, and the vanilla in a medium-sized bowl using electric beaters until pale and fluffy, then add the orange and lime zest, and orange and lime juice, beating until just combined. Sift in flour, baking powder, and poppy seeds, and stir with a wooden spoon to form a soft dough. Divide the mixture into two and wrap each half in plastic wrap. Refrigerate for 1 hour.

Roll out each piece of dough on a lightly floured work surface to form a log. Put on a sheet and fold the parchment paper over to cover the dough and then cover it in plastic wrap and refrigerate for 2 hours.

Preheat the oven to 325°F. Line two cookie sheets with parchment paper.

With a sharp knife, trim the ends and then thinly slice the dough into ¼-inch cookies and place on the sheets 1½ inches apart. Bake for 10–12 minutes, or until lightly golden around the edges. Allow to cool on the sheets for a few minutes, then transfer to a wire rack to cool completely. Repeat with the remaining dough.

These cookies will keep, stored in an airtight container, for up to 2 weeks.

Melting moments with blackberry jam

MAKES 18

1 cup unsalted butter, softened
½ cup confectioners' sugar
1 teaspoon natural vanilla extract
1¾ cups all-purpose flour
½ teaspoon baking powder
½ cup cornstarch
¼ cup confectioners' sugar, extra for dusting
½ cup blackberry jam

Cream filling
¼ cup plus 1 tablespoon unsalted butter, softened
½ cup confectioners' sugar, sifted
½ teaspoon natural vanilla extract

Cream the butter, confectioners' sugar, and vanilla in a medium-sized bowl using electric beaters until pale and fluffy. Sift in the sifted flour, baking powder, and cornstarch, and stir with a wooden spoon until a soft dough forms. Cover with plastic wrap and refrigerate for 1 hour.

To make the cream filling, cream the butter, confectioners' sugar, and vanilla until light and fluffy.

Preheat the oven to 325°F. Line two cookie sheets with parchment paper.

Shape 2 teaspoons of dough into balls and place on the prepared sheets 1½ inches apart. Flatten the balls slightly with a fork dipped in flour and bake for 10–12 minutes, or until lightly golden. Allow to cool on the sheets for a few minutes, then transfer to a wire rack to cool completely. Repeat with the remaining dough.

Dust the cookies with the extra confectioners' sugar. On half of the cookies, place ½ teaspoon of the cream filling. On the other half, place ½ teaspoon of jam. Press together gently to spread the filling to the edge of the cookie.

Filled cookies will keep, stored in an airtight container, for up to 4 days. Unfilled cookies will keep, stored in an airtight container, for 3 weeks.

Florentines

MAKES 12

¼ cup unsalted butter
¼ cup soft brown sugar
2 teaspoons honey
¼ cup flaked almonds, roughly chopped
2 tablespoons chopped dried apricots
2 tablespoons chopped candied cherries
2 tablespoons mixed candied citrus peel
⅓ cup all-purpose flour, sifted
1 cup chopped bittersweet chocolate

Preheat the oven to 350°F. Grease and line two cookie sheets with parchment paper.

Mix the butter, brown sugar, and honey in a saucepan over low heat until the butter is melted and all the ingredients are combined. Remove from the heat and add the almonds, apricots, candied cherries, citrus peel, and the flour. Mix well.

Shape tablespoons of the dough into balls, place on the prepared sheets well apart, and flatten into 2-inch rounds. Bake for 10 minutes, or until lightly browned. Allow to cool on the sheets for a few minutes, then transfer to a wire rack to cool completely.

Place the chocolate in a heatproof bowl over a saucepan of simmering water, ensuring the bowl doesn't touch the water. Stir until the chocolate has melted. Spread the melted chocolate on the bottom of each florentine and, using a fork, make a wavy pattern on the chocolate before it sets. Leave the chocolate to set before serving.

Florentines will keep, stored in an airtight container, for up to 5 days.

Vanilla glazed rings

MAKES 40–44

½ cup unsalted butter, softened
½ cup superfine sugar
2 teaspoons natural vanilla extract
1 small egg, lightly beaten
1¾ cups all-purpose flour
½ teaspoon baking powder
1 quantity frosting glaze (page 90)
yellow food coloring (optional)
1 quantity royal frosting (page 90)

Preheat the oven to 350°F. Lightly grease two cookie sheets.

Cream the butter, sugar, and vanilla in a bowl using electric beaters, then add the egg, beating well. Sift in the flour, baking powder, and a pinch of salt, and stir with a wooden spoon to form a dough.

Break off small pieces of the dough and roll each piece on a lightly floured work surface to form a 4-inch log. Curl into a ring and gently press the ends together. Transfer to the prepared sheets and bake for 10–12 minutes, or until lightly golden. Allow to cool on the sheets for a few minutes, then transfer to a wire rack to cool completely.

Make the frosting glaze, adding a little yellow food coloring (if using) to the glaze. Make the royal frosting and spoon into an frosting bag (or see the tip on page 91 to make your own paper frosting bag).

Using a paintbrush, brush the tops of the cookies with the glaze and leave to set on a wire rack. Pipe the royal frosting backwards and forwards across the cookies to form a zigzag pattern and leave to set.

Vanilla glazed rings will keep, stored in an airtight container, for up to 3 days.

Pecan coffee biscotti

MAKES 40

Preheat the oven to 350°F. Line two cookie sheets with parchment paper.

Place the sifted flour, baking powder, sugar, and a pinch of salt in a food processor and process for 1–2 seconds. Add the butter and mix until the mixture resembles fine breadcrumbs. Add the eggs and vanilla, and process until the mixture is smooth.

Transfer the dough to a well-floured surface and knead in the coffee and pecans. Divide into two equal portions and, using lightly floured hands, shape each into a log about 8 inches long. Place the logs on the cookie sheets and sprinkle with the extra sugar. Press the top of each log down gently to make an oval. Bake for about 35 minutes, or until golden. Remove and set aside to cool for about 20 minutes. Reduce the oven temperature to 325°F.

Cut the logs into ½-inch slices. Turn the parchment paper over and spread the biscotti well apart on the sheet so they don't touch. Return to the oven and bake for a further 30 minutes, or until they just begin to color. Allow to cool on the sheets for a few minutes, then transfer to a wire rack to cool completely.

These biscotti will keep, stored in an airtight container, for up to 3 weeks.

1¾ cups all-purpose flour
½ teaspoon baking powder
⅔ cup superfine sugar
¼ cup unsalted butter
2 eggs
½ teaspoon natural vanilla extract
½ teaspoon instant coffee granules
1⅓ cups whole pecans
½ teaspoon superfine sugar, extra

Tiramisu creams

MAKES 18

½ cup unsalted butter, softened
½ cup confectioners' sugar
1 teaspoon natural vanilla extract
¾ cup all-purpose flour
¼ cup rice flour
¼ cup unsweetened cocoa powder
½ cup ground almonds
2 tablespoons unsweetened cocoa powder,
extra, for dusting

Mascarpone cream
1 tablespoon instant coffee granules
½ cup mascarpone cheese
3 teaspoons confectioners' sugar

Chocolate spread
⅔ cup chopped bittersweet chocolate
1 tablespoon plus 1 teaspoon unsalted butter,
softened
1 tablespoon coffee liqueur

Preheat the oven to 325°F. Line two cookie sheets with parchment paper.

Cream the butter, sugar, and vanilla in a medium-sized bowl using electric beaters. Sift in the flours, cocoa, and almonds, and stir with a wooden spoon to form a soft dough.

Shape teaspoons of the dough into balls, place on the prepared sheets 1½ inches apart and flatten slightly. Bake for 10 minutes. Allow to cool on the sheets for a few minutes, then transfer to a wire rack to cool completely. Repeat with the remaining dough.

To make the mascarpone cream, combine the instant coffee with 1 teaspoon boiling water, stir to dissolve, and allow to cool. Add the mascarpone and sugar.

To make the chocolate spread, place the chocolate in a heatproof bowl over a saucepan of simmering water, ensuring the bowl doesn't touch the water. Stir until the chocolate has melted. Remove from the heat and place in a clean bowl. Allow to cool for a couple of minutes and then add the butter and liqueur, stir, and use immediately.

Spread 1½ teaspoons of the chocolate spread onto half the cookies. Top with 2 teaspoons of mascarpone cream and sandwich with the remaining cookies. Dust with cocoa.

Serve filled cookies immediately. Unfilled cookies will keep, stored in an airtight container, for up to 2 weeks.

Blueberry and almond cookies

MAKES 24

⅓ cup unsalted butter, softened
¾ cup superfine sugar
½ teaspoon almond extract
1 teaspoon natural vanilla extract
1 tablespoon milk
1 cup all-purpose flour
½ teaspoon baking powder
¾ cup ground almonds
⅓ cup dried blueberries
melted white chocolate, for dipping (optional)

Preheat the oven to 350°F. Line two sheets with parchment paper.

Cream the butter, sugar, almond, and vanilla extracts in a medium-sized bowl using electric beaters until pale and fluffy, then add the milk, beating until just combined. Sift in the flour and baking powder, add the ground almonds and blueberries, and stir with a wooden spoon to form a soft dough.

Shape 2 teaspoons of dough into balls, place on the prepared sheets 1½ inches apart, and flatten slightly. Bake for 10–12 minutes, or until lightly golden around the edges. Allow to cool on the sheets for a few minutes, then transfer to a wire rack to cool completely.

These cookies will keep, stored in an airtight container, for up to 2 weeks.

Gingerbread

MAKES 40 (depending on size of cutters)

2⅓ cups all-purpose flour
2 teaspoons baking powder
2 teaspoons ground ginger
heaping ⅓ cup unsalted butter, chilled and diced
¾ cup soft brown sugar
1 egg, beaten
⅓ cup molasses
silver balls (optional)

Frosting glaze
1 egg white
3 teaspoons lemon juice
1¼ cups confectioners' sugar

Royal frosting
1 egg white
scant 1⅔ cups confectioners' sugar

Preheat the oven to 375°F. Lightly grease two cookie sheets.

Sift the flour, baking powder, ground ginger, and a pinch of salt into a bowl. Rub in the butter with your fingertips until the mixture resembles fine breadcrumbs, then stir in the sugar. Make a well in the center, add the egg and molasses and, using a wooden spoon, stir until a soft dough forms. Transfer to a clean surface and knead until smooth.

Divide the dough in half and roll out on a lightly floured work surface until ¼ inch thick. Using various-shaped cookie cutters (hearts, stars, or flowers), cut the dough and then transfer to the prepared sheets. Bake in batches for 8 minutes, or until the gingerbread is light brown. Allow to cool on the sheets for a few minutes, then transfer to a wire rack to cool completely. (If using the gingerbread as hanging decorations, use a skewer to make a small hole in each one while still hot.)

To make the frosting glaze, whisk the egg white and lemon juice together until foamy, then whisk in the confectioners' sugar to form a smooth, thin frosting. Cover the surface with plastic wrap until needed.

To make the royal frosting, lightly whisk the egg white until just foamy, then gradually whisk in enough confectioners' sugar to form a soft frosting. Cover the surface with plastic wrap until needed.

Brush a thin layer of glaze over some of the gingerbread and leave to set. Using an frosting bag (or see the tip below) filled with royal frosting, decorate the gingerbread as shown in the photograph, or as desired.

Gingerbread will keep, stored in an airtight container, for up to 3 days.

TIP: To make a paper frosting bag, cut a piece of parchment paper into a 7½-inch square and then cut in half diagonally to form two triangles. Hold the triangle, with the longest side away from you, and curl the left hand point over and in towards the center.

Repeat with the right hand point, forming a cone shape, with both ends meeting neatly in the middle. Staple together at the wide end. Cut off ½ inch from the tip for the frosting to flow through.

Photograph of recipe is on the front cover.

Amore

MAKES 20

2 cups all-purpose flour
1 teaspoon baking powder
¼ teaspoon pumpkin pie spice
⅓ cup soft brown sugar
½ teaspoon finely grated lemon zest
1 egg
1 tablespoon milk
1 teaspoon natural vanilla extract
heaping ⅓ cup unsalted butter, softened
2 teaspoons unsweetened cocoa powder
1 teaspoon brandy
confectioners' sugar, to dust

Preheat the oven to 325°F. Line two cookie sheets with parchment paper.

Sift the flour, ¼ teaspoon salt, baking powder, and pumpkin pie spice into a bowl. Add the sugar, lemon zest, egg, milk, vanilla, and butter, and, using electric beaters, mix into a smooth dough. Turn out onto a lightly floured surface and roll into a smooth ball. Cover with plastic wrap and refrigerate for 20 minutes.

Divide dough in half. On a lightly floured surface, roll out one portion to ⅛ inch thick. Cut the dough into ten hearts using a 2¾-inch heart-shaped cookie cutter. Re-roll out the scraps and cut out ten ½-inch hearts. Place on the prepared sheets. Working with the other portion, knead in the cocoa and brandy until just combined, then repeat as above.

Lay a small heart onto a large heart of the opposite color. Bake for 12 minutes, or until lightly golden. Allow to cool on the sheets for a few minutes, then transfer to a wire rack to cool completely. Sift over the confectioners' sugar.

These will keep, stored in an airtight container, for up to 5 days.

Index

Thunder Bay Press

An imprint of the Baker & Taylor Publishing Group

10350 Barnes Canyon Road, San Diego, CA 92121

www.thunderbaybooks.com

© 2008 Murdoch Books Pty Limited

All notations of errors or omissions should be addressed to Thunder Bay Press, Editorial Department, at the above address. All other correspondence (author inquiries, permissions) concerning the content of this book should be addressed to Murdoch Books Pty Limited, Pier 8/9, 23 Hickson Road, Sydney NSW 2000, Australia.

ISBN-13: 978-1-60710-227-4
ISBN-10: 1-60710-226-9

Printed in China.

1 2 3 4 5 15 14 13 12 11

IMPORTANT: Those who might be at risk from the effects of salmonella poisoning (the elderly, pregnant women, young children, and those suffering from immune deficiency diseases) should consult their doctor with any concerns about eating raw eggs.

OVEN GUIDE: You may find cooking times vary depending on the oven you are using.
For fan-forced ovens, as a general rule, set the oven temperature to 25°F lower than indicated in the recipe.